SHOPIFY

STEP BY STEP GUIDE ON HOW TO MAKE MONEY ONLINE

TABLE OF CONTENTS

INTRODUCTION

First of all, I want to thank you for taking the time to choose and read my guide on making money with Shopify. This is a beginner's guide and it will walk you through what Shopify is, why you should use it, and how to set up your Shopify account. We will also be looking at some of the very best Shopify apps that you can use as well as delving into the technical side – adding pages, changing the way your Shopify website looks, and how to take payments, as well as all the Shopify plans on offer. Lastly, we look at how you can maximize your earning potential by using Shopify with Amazon and Facebook.

Shopify offers plenty of technical support and advice to help you along your way so even a true beginner can get started in just a short while. By the end of this guide, you will understand what Shopify is and how it can help you in your quest to earn money online.

Really and truthfully, it doesn't matter if you want to earn a bit of extra cash on the side or if you want to be the boss of your own empire, Shopify can help you. There is a kind of appealing side to running a business online, but it isn't without its challenges. It is going to be hard work to start with so don't think you can set this up in minutes and then sit back for an easy ride. You can do it though, provided you have the right ideas, you've done your homework and you are prepared to be in some blood, sweat and tears to do it.

Shopify is now the online store of choice for many entrepreneurs and has been the one method that has helped people to start the online business they always dreamed of starting. And, for those businesses already established, it is a great platform to help them diversify into e-commerce too.

In simple words, if you want a shop, whether you are selling small or are a huge going concern, you can have one with Shopify. And you can customize your store, upload as many products as you want and join the many thousands already making money with Shopify.

Once again, thank you for choosing my guide. Let's get started!

CHAPTER 1

WHAT IS SHOPIFY AND HOW DOES IT WORK?

No doubt you have already heard of Shopify. It is something of a household name now. Unless you have already delved deeply into it then the chances are you won't know what it can do for you and how it works so that's what I'm going to start by telling you before we look at the main advantages and disadvantages of using it.

So, what is it?

Shopify is a way of setting up a store online, providing you with an easy platform to sell just about anything that you want. It is incredibly popular with entrepreneurs and businesses who want an easy way to create an e-commerce shop that can operate alone or as part of an existing company.

One thing that sets Shopify aside from the competition is the fact that it is incredibly versatile. You don't need to have any experience in writing code. If all you want is a simple store to get up and running pretty much straight away, Shopify has a range of templates that you can choose from. These provide the skeleton of the store and can be customized so you can put your own unique stamp on your store. However, Shopify is not limited to small businesses or internet entrepreneurs; it is scalable, customizable and even multi-lingual, making it the perfect platform for any business even the biggest of brands like Red Bull, KKW Beauty, WaterAid and Budweiser – all using Shopify as their online store platform.

How does it Work?

Shopify is dead simple to use, one of the biggest reasons why it is so popular. It is a web-based software so there is no need to install it first. The platform is fully hosted by Shopify and this brings several advantages, including full customer support. There isn't any need to go through complex installations, worry about upgrades that might mess things up and you don't need to worry about any web servers – it's all done for you. And Shopify is compatible with all the major operating systems.

Setting up a store is simple, as you will see later. All you need to do is sign up for your free 14-day trial on Shopify and give it a go. Once the free trial period is up you need to decide whether to continue or not and which plan to choose. We'll be looking at those plans later on, but there are several to choose from, each with its own unique features and price. Then, you just need to decide on what to sell and add your payment details to pay for your subscription.

That's all there is to it. You can register a domain name so your Shopify store has the name you want it to have and if you already have a website or a domain name, simply integrate it all with Shopify - I'll show you how later.

Shopify Advantages

Shopify has several decent advantages and one of the biggest is that it offers more than 100 different themes for you to choose from for your storefront. This allows you to choose a professional look that also looks good on a mobile device. For those that have used WordPress, the approach to Shopify themes is quite similar – a store holds the themes and you can browse to choose what you want. Some are free, some require payment and you can also choose from themes set up for specific industries. These themes have been professionally designed and Shopify ensures that they consistent and compatible with its own software before they allow them into the store.

Another great advantage is the flexibility that Shopify offers, allowing to use the Shopify app store to add different functionalities. There are over 1200 apps to choose from and we'll be looking at some of them in a later chapter. Again, some of them are free while some are paid and you can pick and choose the ones that help make your store easier to use and to automate certain aspects of it. There are social media apps, customer service, inventory management, accounting, even shipping apps, all available to add to your store to help run your new business. All of this makes Shopify more than a simple store; it is a complete business solution, providing assistance for the backend as well as the frontend. And if you worried about installing the apps, don't be because Shopify will do the work for you.

If there is one thing designed to send people into a panic, it's a glitch that causes their website to go down with no warning and leaving them with no idea how to get it all back again. Shopify is robust but, to deal with any issues that arise and any problems you may have their next advantage is that they operate a 24/7 customer support service. They offer several different phone numbers for different areas, they have email support and online chat so your problems can be solved straight away. Time is money as any business owner knows and the minimum amount of fuss and maximum speed to get an issue resolved is crucial.

The Shopify software is in the cloud so you have a great deal more flexibility because any web browser can be used to run it. You can work wherever you want, whenever you want, as long as you have a connection to the internet.

Security is not an issue either; Shopify does it all for you, ensuring all transactions are completely secure so you can concentrate on selling your goods.

Lastly, there is a Shopify POS (point of sale) app for both Android and iOS that helps take care of in-person transactions. Using it means you can sell anywhere – at a market, a fair, in a popup window, anywhere you want. Plus it offers the versatility of accepting multiple methods of payment. The best of it is, the app fully syncs with your account so your orders can be monitored as can stock levels in real time, across all your points of sale – online, physical store, and so on.

Shopify Disadvantages

While Shopify has plenty of advantages, it also has a few disadvantages. Don't be too surprised; nothing is perfect and nothing can possibly suit everyone so make sure you are aware of the downsides before you start.

Unless you make use of the Shopify payments system, you will need to pay a fee on each sale and that can be anywhere from 0.5% to 2%, depending on which plan you are signed up to. If you opt for the basic plan, the transaction fee is 2% of each sale; the Shopify Plan is 1% and the Advanced Plan is 0.5%. How much of a disadvantage this proves to be is down to your perspective. In terms of money, it is equal to between $0.50 and $2 for every $100 sale – that isn't too bad and that money is used to pay for the payment management technology that Shopify uses. In simple terms, all you are doing is paying them to handle your transactions. Plus, Shopify doesn't hide their fees; they are completely upfront and you will always know what the charges are going to be.

Not all the apps are free to use. While they can offer huge amounts of functionality, some of them do have a monthly cost attached to them and this can soon bump up your monthly expenditure. Take MailChimp, for example, a popular mail app that helps you to run a mail campaign. If you have less than 2000 email subscribers then Mailchimp is free, but any more and the costs are anywhere between $10 and $200 per month. Another one, FreshBooks, is a great accounting app but it will set you back almost $32 a month.

As far as apps go, if you have a small business most of them are free. But, grow your business larger and you may have to start paying out for those apps. For someone like you who is going to be starting a brand-new business, for now, you won't need to worry about that. And, if your business does grow, your revenue should grow with it and those all-important apps won't seem quite so expensive. You could try doing the accounting and marketing yourself to start with, but you will find that your attention will be on that and not on selling. You could also hire an external person to do for you, but that will definitely cost you more than the app would. Perhaps, in the long run, the best option is to bit the bullet and buy the app, saving yourself the time that you could be using to focus on selling.

Many platforms make use of CSS or HTML coding, but Shopify doesn't. Instead, it uses something called Liquid so store customization means you need to know the language or you need to know someone who does. That can prove expensive so, to begin with, stick with the themes on offer and leave the customization for later down the line.

While Shopify is incredibly flexible, and it can be highly customized, some parts of it can't unless you opt for the very expensive Shopify Plus plan so be aware of that from the start.

So, as you can see, most of the disadvantages revolve around costs and expense but, if you want a successful business, those are inevitable – you can't have it all for nothing. If you had a physical store, for example, you would have overheads in rent and utilities, not to mention taxes, staff, inventory and so on. With Shopify, the monthly subscription you choose is akin to these costs but much cheaper.

Let's move on and look at the different plans Shopify offers.

CHAPTER 2

THE DIFFERENT SHOPIFY PLANS

Now you know what Shopify is and how it works, let's take a look at what plans are on offer. Which one you choose will be determined by how large your business is and what your requirements are. There are five plans to choose from:

- Basic Shopify
- Shopify
- Advanced Shopify
- Shopify Lite
- Shopify Plus

Before we look at each one in a little more detail, bear in mind that Shopify offers domains for $9 a month. There are also monthly and yearly options for payment and you can upgrade or downgrade whenever you want with no charge. The only difference will be the difference in the payments. If this is your first time with Shopify, you are better off starting with monthly payments. There are no cancellation charges when you are paying annually, but you also won't get a refund of any unused portion of the payment. Test things out first by paying monthly – you won't lose so much if things don't work out.

The Plans

When you land on the Shopify page detailing their plans you will only see the first three options from the list above. You will find the Lite and Plus plans detailed at the bottom of the page. Lite is the cheapest plan and Plus is the most expensive. A quick rundown of what you can expect to pay:

- Shopify Lite - $9/month
- Basic Shopify - $29/month
- Shopify - $79/month
- Advanced Shopify - $299/month
- Shopify Plus – prices start at about $2000 per month but are variable.

Each of the plans also has their own credit card rates and these are what you will get charged if you choose the Shopify Payments option to manage transactions and payment processes. Basically, when a purchase is made from your Shopify store, you get charged by the payment processor – the system that collects your money and places it onto your bank. Credit card rates are handling fees for transferring money from the purchases to the seller. These are normal and you cannot avoid paying them – at the end of the day, it means you don't need to meet every one of your customers in person, collect the cash and then deposit it into your own bank account.

Let's delve into the plans.

Shopify Lite

At $9 a month, Shopify Lite is the cheapest plan and it provides only the very basic features, such as:

- A Facebook selling channel
- Payment tools – for credit card and other forms of payment
- A couple of Buy buttons.

It is advertised separately to the main plans because, technically, it isn't really an online store. Instead, it provides access to a couple of features that can be added to an existing website, blog or social media account, enabling you to sell on a small scale. It also has a neat feature that allows you to connect Facebook Messenger on your Facebook business page to your account on Shopify. This lets you chat instantly with your customers and provide a very quick solution for customer support.

If you do not have a website or a blog already set up and doing well then Shopify Lite isn't for you. The idea behind Lite is so that it can be added to an existing online platform that already has its own domain and hosting in place. It's perfect if you have those platforms and just want to sell a few items – installing Shopify Lite to your website is really quite simple.

Shopify Basic

Shopify Basic costs $29 per month and this one will provide you with an online store with lots of useful features. These features include:

- An engine for discount codes
- Uploading as many items as you want to your store
- Tools for fraud analysis
- Unlimited storage for files
- 24/7 technical support
- SSL certificate for encryption and security
- Manual order creation

The plan also comes with a blog and a website, ensuring that everything is linked together as it should be and fully managed through Shopify. You get everything you need to create an online store that is fully functional and looks professional. The store can be used whether you have a website or blog or not.

The credit card rate is 2.9% plus $0.30 for each transaction on top of the monthly fee.

Shopify

This is the middle plan and is, so far, the most popular. It is, however, $79 per month, a fair bit more than the Basic plan. The reason it is so popular is that it offers pretty much every Shopify feature you could possibly need.

You get everything the Basic plan offers plus some extras, including:

- Professional reports
- Recovery for abandoned carts
- A gift card feature

The abandoned cart tool is quite useful because it stores all the information from those who visit, start adding to the shopping cart but don't finish off their order. By retaining their information, you can then contact the customer later – they were obviously interested enough to start shopping so you can try to encourage them to finish. However, instead of you needing to make contact with each of these customers individually, you also have the tools to automate the process by automatically sending a customized email to them. You can even decide when the email should be sent, from a matter of hours after they abandon the shopping cart to days.

Why is this such an important feature? Simply because research has shown that almost 70% of online customers abandon their cart before completing a purchase but, when they are contacted later, they often end up spending up to 50% more. This isn't just good for gaining sales, it also helps you to determine why the initial sales are not being completed. Perhaps your store is a bit confusing or the purchasing process takes too long and customers give up. These are all things you need to know so you can put them right and make things easier for customers.

If you are thinking about growing your business quickly then the features of this plan, such as unlimited storage and unlimited products are great. This plan is also ideal for those who already earn more than $5,000 a month through online sales – the transaction fee is cheaper than the Basic. Plus, the abandoned cart recovery feature is worth paying a bit more for because it could potentially increase your earnings quite significantly.

The credit card rate is 2.6% and $0.30 per transaction.

Advanced Shopify

Costing $299 a month, Advanced Shopify is not cheap, but it does offer quite a few advantages for the large businesses. As well as everything from the Basic Plan and the Shopify Plan, Advanced also offers pretty much unlimited everything:

- Unlimited product uploads
- Unlimited storage capacity
- Unlimited uploads for posts and videos
- Unlimited abandoned cart recovery package
- Shipping discounts
- Advanced reporting
- Adding access for up to 15 different users

The money saved on the shipping discounts and transaction fees make this the ideal plan for a business earning $10,000 or more every month. It also allows for shipping to be taken care of by another party and provides business reports that offer more detail so you can analyze data, test out different variables for marketing and try to make projections for the future.

The credit card rate is 2.4% plus $0.30 per transaction.

Shopify Plus

The final plan is Shopify Plus, the plan that proves this is more than just a platform for selling small amounts of simple goods. This is for the big companies and organizations and it provides management for all orders and operations for every sale. You also get 200 TB storage capacity, more than enough for even the largest store and the biggest benefit is no transaction fees.

However, you can't sign up for this plan through the website. Instead, you must call Shopify direct and discuss your requirements with them to get a quote. The minimum fee is $2,000 per month though.

This is a highly customizable option giving you the opportunity to adapt it to your branding and requirement; the level of technical and customer support is excellent, as it should be when you fork out that kind of cash every month, and you get a dedicated account manager working with you all the way.

The Shopify Plus platform can handle large visitor volumes easily, and there are no issues with processing potentially thousands of sales every minute, making this the ideal plan for the largest of businesses. It's ideal for the company that wants to concentrate on sales, customer service, and marketing, automating the rest as far as possible and leaving it to a third party to deal with.

How Do You Choose a Plan?

That is going to come down to a few factors, such as your monthly budget and the size of your company. If you run a blog and want to sell just a few products per month through your own website then the Lite plan will be sufficient.

If you have a store already but with another provider, Shopify helps you to make the transfer easily. The other way to determine which plan is right for you is to use the data you already have on sales, customers, stock, and so on.

CHAPTER 3

SHOPIFY FEATURES

We mentioned some of the features that are available on each of the plans so now we'll look at them in a little more detail.

Features for Every Plan:

Every Shopify Plan comes with these features:

- **Unlimited Products –** you can upload unlimited products to your store with no restrictions

- **Unlimited Bandwidth/Unlimited Storage -** this is important. You can have as many visitors as you like and upload as many videos and photos as you want without being charged any extra

- **Shopify POS –** this is the Point-of-Sale feature, a neat tool that lets you make sales at a physical store, be it a market, fair, or so on. The POS app must be installed to your Android or iOS device and you can then process

14

sales and transactions anywhere you want, as well as managing your store from within your Shopify account

- **Channel for Online Sales** – with this, you can use several sales channels – your Shopify store, social media accounts, and so on. Everything is seamlessly integrated so you can manage everything in one place, monitoring orders, transactions and everything across all channels.

- **Fraud Analysis** – this is added in Shopify Payments automatically, helping you to track potentially fraudulent orders and alerting you to any risks. This ensures your transactions are legitimate and you avoid losses.

- **Discount Codes** – discount codes are a good way of enticing people into your store, building up a bigger audience and more potential sales. If you use Instagram, you may have spotted one or two influencers who provide fans with unique codes to use with specific brands. Well, these are the codes that the Shopify plans give you. How you give them to your audience is entirely up to you; you could ask influencers or bloggers to give your store a bit of promotion in exchange for something, you could give the codes out to first-time buyers to give them some kind of incentive or you could use them in a targeted email drive – it's up to you.

- **Overview** - each plan provides you with an overview of your key sales data. This will tell you your overall sales numbers, how many visitors your store gets, how many orders are placed and so on. You are also provided with finance reports showing your income, expenditure and any transactions that are pending.

- **Customer Service** – Shopify provides you with several ways to contact them and they are operational 24/7. With the Lite plan you get an email address and Live Chat, with all others you also get phone numbers to call them on.

- Those are the features on every plan; let's look at what the other features are:

The Basic Plan

- These features are not available on Lite but are available on the Shopify and the Advanced Plans:

- **Online Store -** this is a platform that is customizable to your requirements and used for displaying and selling your products. It is, in essence, the only way that your customers see your brand and the only place where you can track every order, transaction, all your products, stock levels and customer information for your store. It has a blog and website built into it so these can be run beside your store, ensuring your products are linked to great content that tells your audience what you are selling, to reach out to new customers and get some much-needed feedback.

- **SSL Certificate -** this tool ensures that you and your customers have a secure connection between the browser and the server. Your information is safe as are the details your customers provide. When activated, a small SSL padlock shows in the address bar, telling your customers they are visiting a secure site.

The Shopify Plan

As well as the features on the Basic plan, this plan also has a few extras that the basic plan doesn't have. These extras can make all the difference in the brand experience you give your customers:

- **Gift Cards** – discount codes are good, but gift cards go the extra step. Where a discount code is valid for one visit, gift cards can be used on multiple visits to your store. It is also a good way of getting new customers as your existing ones can buy them as gifts for friends and family who then go on to become a customer of yours. Shopify has different prices for gift cards so your customers get the flexibility of choice. As well as that, you get the ability to show off your branding by customizing the gift card.

- **Professional Reports** – these are helpful in letting you analyze the way your customers make purchases. They show sales by product, helping you to organize your store format better, to prepare for changes that are seasonal and pan your marketing and ad campaigns. You also see information about your customers and the way they interact with your Shopify store. For example, you will see how many first-time visitors you have had, return customers, customers by country, one-off or repeated purchases and more.

- **Abandoned Cart Recovery** – we talked about his in the last chapter. If your budget allows, it is definitely worth upgrading your plan to get this feature because it can potentially increase your sales quite significantly. This is an especially helpful feature for high-traffic stores.

The Advanced Shopify Plan

- In addition to the features on the Basic and Shopify plans, the Advanced Plan also offers these features:

- **Custom Report Builder** - with this, you can make reports that are customized and unique, allowing you a better understanding of what happens on your site. For example, if you have an ad campaign on the go to try to increase traffic, you can get a report that tracks that campaign by linking it to traffic and relevant sales. This is great for testing the performance of campaigns and using the data to create new strategies.

- **Calculated Carrier Shipping** – finally, you get a feature that allows for the integration of other shipping services into your store. This is beneficial in two ways – first, the shopping rates are exact when a customer makes a purchase and, second, you shoppers get a choice of delivery options, including one-day, express and standard.

Other Features

- While that covers the main features of each plan, there are a few others that may not be aware of in Shopify:

- **Customer Profiles** – customers can be asked to create an account before they can start shopping. With this, you can track all their transactions, works out your best customers and what they are buying. Why would you need to know this? So that your email and marketing campaigns can be customized, so you can set up loyalty rewards for the best customers, and you can use their purchase history to send them emails. For example, let's say a customer purchased a special daytime moisturizing cream from you. You could email them when you estimate that they will be running out of it, giving them the chance to make another purchase.

- **Shopify With Facebook** - This is a great feature for those who have large Facebook followings. When you integrate Shopify with Facebook, your customers can make their purchase directly from your Facebook page without needing to open your site. This is easier and convenient for the customers and these are deciding factors in making or breaking sales. Facebook will also sync to Shopify, ensuring your transactions are updated on both platforms.

- **Drop-Shipping** – you can also use your Shopify store to do drop-shipping. This way, you can sell the products without having to purchase them first. A customer will make a purchase from your store; the order is sent to a third-party supplier; they send the product out to the customer. The customer won't know where the product is coming from and you get to save money on inventory costs.

- **Future Publishing** – to help with time management, future publishing allows you to line up content for publishing on set days and times in the future. The content won't show until that specified date and time. You can spend time writing weeks or months' worth of work, which can be published when you want it to, saving time later down the line.

- **Two-Step Authentication** – your store will be secure from hackers who might be able to steal passwords and other sensitive data. Even if a hacker did manage to get your password, the two-factor authentication would make it hard for them to get into your about as they would not be able to verify the login through the code sent to your mobile phone, And, if you get a code out of the blue, you'll know that a hacker is lurking.

CHAPTER 4

WHY USE SHOPIFY?

So, who benefits from using Shopify? Anyone who wants to run a business with a minimum amount of hassle, for a start. If you went to a hotel and the hot water wasn't working, you would call the front desk and report it; they would have to fix it. If you are the hotel owner, it's down to you to fix things; running a Shopify store is running the hotel!

Let's say that you have kids and, while they are at school, you need something to do with your time. A Shopify store will give you that something as well as potentially earning you the money to contribute to the household. In the same way, college students could earn some extra income.

If you already have a product but don't know how to go about selling it, Shopify is ideal. It provides you the all-inclusive e-commerce platform you need to get your products up for sale online.

And lastly, if you already have a fulltime job but really want to be your own boss, Shopify is a great starting point. Obviously, you shouldn't ditch your job straightaway but using Shopify will give you an idea of whether you can make enough money to go it alone.

Why You Should Choose Shopify:

- It's not expensive and because it's so easy to use you get to focus on selling without having to worry about maintaining a website

- There are tons of designs and layouts for your store, all provided by Shopify, and many of them are completely free. If you want a new look every couple of months you can have one. If you need something more specialized, the Shopify design pros will do it for you – at a cost of course.

- Any changes to your site can be made discoverable by all the big search engines. You have an unmatched ability to put in whatever information you want, such as titles, descriptions, and so on. This helps you to make your store SEO-friendly.

- If you need help, it's there, 24/7. Things happen that are outside of our control and a bit of technical help is needed to get things back up and running quickly, providing you with complete peace of mind.

- Internet security is a huge concern with online shoppers these days and we hear far too many stories about identity theft and credit card fraud. Both you and your shop customers can be reassured that Shopify spends a lot of money on security, using SSL and HTTPS to keep their site secure.

- You can spend as little as $29 a month to run a Shopify store. Shopify keep their prices affordable so that pretty much anyone can have their own store.

- Shopify gives you everything you need to get off and running very quickly, just minutes in some cases. You need little in the way of technical experience or skills and complete beginners can use Shopify with ease. Start small and grow or choose your plan and stay put, it's up to you.

- Shopify offers more than online stores. You can also join in if you run a physical store using the Shopify POS app, a complete package that requires no third party to be involved.

Before we start looking at how to set up your Shopify online store, we'll take a quick look at some of the best apps that Shopify offers to help you with your business.

CHAPTER 5

TOP SHOPIFY APPS

Shopify is, without a doubt, a great e-commerce platform. It is affordable, it is easy to use and you can get set up and running right out of the box in a very short time. It isn't just a storefront; you get checkouts that are fully featured so retailers can begin taking payments from their customers straight away and Shopify Shipping makes fulfilling orders a breeze, managing the entire process for you. And Shopify also has the tools to deal with marketing for you – you can have automated emails sent and Shopify can even come up with targeted social marketing campaigns.

Basically, Shopify makes starting an e-commerce business and growing it very simple. If you want an online store or you want to move an already-existing online store to a more user-friendly platform, then Shopify is a great choice. However, while it offers all you need to get your store off the ground, you can make things a good deal better by using some of the add-ons that Shopify offers in the form of apps. We're going to look at some of the best apps you can use with your Shopify store:

- **Edit Order**

Edit Order is designed to help you edit completed orders, which means altering orders that were placed incorrectly (wrong size, wrong color, etc.). You can also change billing addresses, and order prices, as well as streamlining your policy for returns. The app is $14.99 per month with a 14-day free trial.

- **Audience Push**

This is a vital app for any Shopify store owner who also uses Facebook for advertising. Once your Facebook account is connected to Shopify (a single-click achieves that) Audience Push updates the Facebook Custom Audience List automatically with all new customer information. This can save you a huge amount of time. The app is $9 per month with a 14-day free trial.

- **Order Printer**

The ability to print receipts, orders and packaging labels is a vital part of any e-commerce store, but this is not a standard part of Shopify. That means Order Printer is a crucial app. The document design and layout is completely customizable and you can also print in bulk to save some time. This is a free app.

- **Persistent Cart**

Persistent Cart is one of the easiest apps to install and can save sales for you. If a customer leaves your site without going through checkout, the app will save their cart. That cart will then be available, exactly as it was, when they come back, even if they are using a different device. There is a free version of the app, but it doesn't offer anywhere near the features of the paid app which costs just $3.99 per month with a 30-day free trial.

- **Google Shopping**

Google Shopping is one of the in-house apps that help you to up your sales without too much effort. It works by automating the way you list products on Google Shopping or the way they are listed as Product Listing Ads. Once you connect it, the app syncs your store automatically with the Google Merchant Center, allowing listings to be updated from right within Shopify. The app is free to install, but there may be additional charges.

- **Tidio Live Chat**

Most customers want instant communication with a company and demand a Live Chat feature on a website. This is because they can get an answer to their question straightaway, improving efficiency and better levels of customer satisfaction. Tidio enables integration of Live Chat though their plugin and the app is free although additional charges may apply.

- **Exit Offers**

The Exit Offers app can help to increase your sales by saving customers that are about to leave your site without making a purchase. When they add products to the shopping cart and then go to leave without finishing, you can show them an offer that is designed to make them want to buy. That offer is down to you, but it could be a certain percentage off their order, free shipping, or something like it. The app costs $9.99 per month with a 14-day free trial.

- **Orderify**

Orderify gives your customers better control over what they purchase. They can edit their orders, cancel them (provided they haven't been shipped) and even reorder previous purchases very easily, leading to happy customers and more sales. The app costs $4.99 per month with a 30-day free trial.

- **McAfee SECURE**

Most customers prefer to make their purchases from a store they can trust and if they feel at all uncomfortable about adding their card details to your site, they won't do it. McAfee SECURE is a widget that provides that element of trust, showing your customers that they can trust your site 100%. The app is free, but additional charges may apply.

- **Oberlo**

Oberlo is a great little app for helping you to find a product for selling or a business idea. Using Oberlo, search a marketplace containing products that can be directly imported to your Shopify store. When an order comes in, Oberlo ships straight to your customers, eliminating the need for you to worry about packaging the goods and shipping them. This is a free app, but additional charges may apply.

- **Klaviyo**

Klaviyo provides you with a very powerful package for email marketing automation at business-level speeds. One click integrates Klaviyo with your Shopify store and you can easily set up autoresponders, such as an email about abandoned carts, welcome emails, follow-ups on order and so on. The app is free to download.

- **Product Reviews**

With Shopify Product Reviews, you can add a feature to your products for customers to leave reviews. This way, your customers get another way of engaging with you and with each other, a great way of encouraging sales. This is a free app.

- **Plug in SEO**

Plug In SEO is an app that shows you at a glance if there are any SEO issues with your site that need to be fixed. The app will check the homepage of your store and display its verdict, providing details of where fixes need to be made. The app has a free plan available and 7-day completely free trial.

- **Facebook Store**

With Facebook Store you can show off your products on your Facebook page and sell them too. Your customers can share products with their follower, friends and family and you get a much wider reach in terms of audience and traffic. The app is free to install.

- **Bulk Discounts**

With Bulk Discounts you can import discount codes directly to your store or you can create them to dish out to your customers. This is a free app.

- **Free Shipping Bar**

Free Shipping Bar provides you with a slide bar that you can use for showing offers for free shipping. It can also show messages as customers add items to their carts and congratulate your customers on getting the free shipping offer. This is free to install, but there are other similar apps that may offer more and charge a small monthly fee.

- **ALT Text**

ALT Tet generates the ALT text for the images in your store automatically. This will be based on a specified parameter set and is designed to drive more traffic your way from the search engines. The app costs $1.99 per month.

- **Yotpo**

Yotpo is a useful app that helps you to easily generate reviews for your products. These can then be shared across your social media profiles to help drive more traffic and more potential sales. It is free to install, but there are priced plans available for premium business customers.

- **Printful**

With the Printful app, you can sync with your store for drop shipping custom products like printed t-shirts, mugs, etc. The order come via your store and goes to Printful to print and ship for you. This is a free app.

- **Improved Contact Form**

With Improved Contact Form you can create a contact form that pops up in your store, telling you the location of the customer and which pages they looked at before they made contact with you. It is a free app, but additional charges may apply.

- **Better Coupon Box**

Better Coupon Box is designed to help you covert all visitors to your store into potential customers. When a customer goes into your store for the first time, they will see a gorgeous popup that offers them a specific discount if they follow you on your Twitter, Facebook, or other social media profiles. This is a free app.

- **AfterShip**

With AfterShip, you can keep track of every shipment in one central place and let your customers have regular delivery updates. Support is provided for more than 350 carriers including UPS, DHL, FedEx, USPS, and more. There is a free plan although more features are offered with paid plans and there is a 14-day free trial.

- **eBay Professional Importer**

This app takes the catalog from your eBay store and copies it over to your Shopify store. All products are supported, including active, unsold and scheduled and will also handle all the images, categories, and variations automatically. The app starts at $14.95 per month and there is a 30-day free trial.

- **Shippo**

Shippo allows you to integrate all orders on your Shopify store and print shipping labels with a single click. You can choose the dimensions of your parcels, data for pickup, type of service, your preferred carrier, and so on and your labels are provided within seconds. The app is free to install, but there may be additional charges.

- **Social Media Stream**

Social Media Stream lets you showcase your Twitter, Facebook, Instagram, Pinterest, YouTube and Tumblr posts on one page, helping you to get more followers on your social media accounts and cut down the time you have to spend embedding posts and images. There is a free plan available, but additional charges may apply.

- **Digital Downloads**

Digital Downloads gives you the opportunity to include digital products in your store. Customers can have instant access to the content and any updates to the products are sent to the customers automatically. This is a free app.

There are thousands more apps to choose from, but these will give you a good head start in making the most of your Shopify store. Although your budget may dictate that you only go for the free apps, do bear in mind that the paid versions of apps tend to offer more features and, to be fair, provided you do your marketing, the money you pay out can be recouped pretty quickly.

CHAPTER 6

SETTING UP YOUR SHOPIFY STORE

Setting your store up is actually quite easy once you know which features you want to use so that's what we are going to do now – set up the store, add a product and come up with a URL that will allow your customers to recognize you online.

Choose Your Platform

First, you must work out which service and platform you want to use. Let's see what the services are first. Well, this applies to the pricing plans we looked at in an earlier chapter. Most of these are pretty much identical in features, but the more expensive plans have more advanced features. And don't forget that credit card fee per transaction on top of the monthly fee for the service.

For those just getting their foot in the door, the lowest service is probably the best as it gives you a chance to test the waters and learn how things work before you upgrade. Once you get a handle on the basics and the money starts rolling in, you can choose to upgrade. Keep in mind that the Basic Shopify plan does come with quite a bit though.

Your next decision is which platform you want to use and by this, I am talking about the website you want your Shopify Store to be connected to. You can, if you choose, connect your store to several platforms at once so let's see which ones are available:

Facebook:

Facebook has a built-in store option and when Shopify is connected, your page will allow customers to either visit your store or purchase from right there on your Facebook page. If you have a page that is often shared, this can be a great idea because you get access to a wider audience who can see your products instantly and decide whether they want to buy straight away and see what else you have for sale. This works for those who have a large following on the social media platform.

Pinterest Buttons:

Pinterest is still one of the biggest social media sites and quite easily outpaces Twitter in user participation and growth so it should not be pushed to the wayside. Shopify partners with Pinterest so you can link product pins to your Shopify account, allowing customers to buy instantly. Even better, the purchase takes place in the Pinterest app so your customers don't have to jump through a ton of hoops to get access to your products – this can increase your sales percentage quite significantly.

Shopify Store:

Shopify provides space in their store for you to set up an online shop. They have a drag-and-drop interface that helps you to create a great-looking storefront. The upside to this system is that is easy and eliminates the need to spend hours working on designing and building a website. Shopify provides strong support for their sales platform and they also offer app support for WordPress and other websites. Shopify has all the customization you want to get a great store up and running in just minutes.

Your Own Website:

WordPress and Squarespace are good options for websites, but they don't really work too well with Shopify. Shopify has put a lot of hard work in to come up with their own platform and, while you could use WordPress, it takes a lot of work and a knowledge of coding to integrate Shopify. You also won't be able to use the apps n the Shopify stores. We'll be starting by using the Shopify platform as it is much easier so let's get started.

1. Go to http://www.shopify.com and sign up for your free trial account. Input your email address and then click on Get Started.

2. Create a password and note it down so you can remember it.

3. Input your store name. If you don't really have one yet just type in anything; you can change it again later.

4. Click on Create Your Store

5. Next, you need to decide if it's an online store you want or you want to sell in a pop-up store or a physical store. For now, choose an online store because that will provide you with a website to sell your goods from.

6. Click on Next and then input your name and address. These details are used for setting up your Shopify account so they won't show up in your store. Your store details will be set up later.

7. Click the button for "This Is My Retail Store Address" ONLY if you want to use the name and address you input as your store address; if not, leave the box unticked.

8. Click on "Take Me To My Store." Nobody can see your store yet because it has been protected by a password and only those with the password can see it. You only remove that password when you are ready for your store to go live.

9. Now your store admin area is created. At the top of the browser window you will see a URL. Bookmark the page or write the URL down. This is your admin area, where your entire store is controlled. Click on "View Your Website" at the top of the screen and you will see your store.

That's it and your store is created and you are ready to start adding products.

CHAPTER 7

ADDING YOUR PRODUCTS

Right now, your store is looking a little bit empty so let's add a product and see what it looks like.

1. Click on "Back to Dashboard" so you go back to the Admin area and then click on "Add Products."

2. Pick a product that you have an image for already and type a descriptive title in into the text box for Title

3. Under the description, a number of fields will appear; fill them in with the correct details – these can be changed later so input anything for now.

4. Obviously, "Price" is what the product will be sold at and "Compare At Price" shows you what you sold the product for previously – this can be left blank if it doesn't apply to you.

5. Either input an SKU – a stock keeping unit – or leave it empty so one can be assigned. If you have an ISBN, an ASIN, or a barcode, the details go in the Barcode field. This lets the search engines easily index products, adding them, in Google's case, to their price comparison feature.

6. Lastly, decide if you are keeping an inventory and whether the "Out of Stock" option should be shown by Shopify so you don't sell any more than currently in stock. You can leave the box for "Multiple Options" blank for now.

7. Now click "Choose Files" and add some images of the product.

8. For the "Visibility" option choose visible so you can see your store with your newly added products. Once you have seen it, you can delete the product or make it invisible but, once again, because your website is password protected, nobody can see it or buy the product.

9. Click on "Save Product" and choose to "View in Website" – button at the top of the page.

Doesn't that look good? Add a few more products and then we'll move on to setting up your domain and emails.

CHAPTER 8

DOMAINS AND EMAILS

Before your store goes live there are a few other details you need to deal with and the first is your domain name. When you choose one of the three main plans you get given a domain name but it isn't very exciting and it will do nothing for your credibility online. All that domain name consists of is your name followed by .shopify.com. You need a domain that is going to scream your brand or your product from the rooftops and Shopify helps you to do this by letting you buy a domain name through a domain registrar. When you purchase through an external registrar, that name is yours for as long as you choose, even if you, one day, decide to move on from Shopify.

Use a reputable domain registrar, like GoDaddy. You will find that most offer much the same service but do your homework thoroughly and don't forget to read the small print!

Once you have chosen your domain registrar, type in the domain name you want and click on Search. You will see a list of the domain names that match or come somewhere near what you typed in. If the name has already been taken, you will need to think of another – tip: before you go looking for a registrar, spend some time thinking of several names that will suit your business. It's highly unlikely that you will get the one you really want!

Your name needs to be memorable, not too long and easy to spell. People don't like complicated website names and will tend to move on to an easier one! You should pay no more than about $15 a year for a domain name if it is not a premium com or co.uk name – these will set you back a little more.

Chose which name you want and click on the "Checkout button" and decide how long a term you want to pay for. Longer periods tend to work out cheaper per year and 2 years seems to be the best bet – it's long enough to give your business chance to shine but doesn't tie you in for too long.

Input your payment and address details but be aware; if people search Whois for your domain name this address will show up. If you don't want your address made public, you can pay for an extra privacy feature on most registrars.

Once you have successfully ordered and paid for your domain name, you get a confirmation email. Click on the link in the email and you will be redirected to your control panel. Now you are ready to add that name to your Shopify site.

Return to the Shopify dashboard and click the option for the "Domains" menu. Click "Add an Existing Domain." Type your new domain name in and click "Add Domain." On your screen you will see a DNS address – write this down, you will need it in a minute. Also, write down the URL from the address bar – yourdomainname.myshopify.com.

In the control panel for your domain name (whichever registrar you chose), click on the option for "Manage Domains." Choose your domain name from the dropdown list and then go to the top of the page. Click on DNS and scroll through the list, clicking on "Show Advanced DNS Options."

Click to "Add a New Record" and type in the DNS number you wrote down – it must be exact, something along the lines of 205.95.223.56 (not this number!). In the Host box, type in your domain name, omitting the www from it. TTL needs to be set to 300.

Repeat these steps with CNAME and input your domain information.

It will take a while for all this to start working but, when they do, you will be able to use your own domain name to access your Shopify store.

Back in the dashboard for your Shopify store, click on "Domains" and then on "Set as Primary." Click on "Save" and you are ready to move on to the next step.

Setting up your Email Account

Now that your domain is all set up it's time to look at emails. You need a minimum of one email account for the domain name and this can be used for all your Shopify store contact details. Later on, you can set up one for each department or person in your business if you want. When you purchase your domain name, the registrar will likely provide you with one email address and a number of forwarders so what you could do is set up a primary email account and use other addresses to forward emails to that main account. If you need extra mailboxes, you can buy upgrades.

In your domain registrar control panel, click on "Email" and then on "Add New Address." Where it says Account Name, type in what you want the email address to be, sticking with a generic name for now like sales or mail. This becomes your primary address.

Next, click on "Add New Forwarder" and input the addresses you require, forwarding them to the primary email address you created first.

Once your email account has been set up, you can use any email client to access them, but the easiest way is to use the client supplied by your domain account. So, find your main email account and click "Login" beside it. Input your email and your password and then click on "Compose."

Input a message, with a subject line and an email address to send it to – use your own personal one for this test – and click on "Send." Check your personal email account to make sure the email came through. Reply to it and then go back to your domain email account to make sure the reply came through okay. If it did, all is working well.

Now we can move on to setting up the remainder of your Shopify store.

CHAPTER 9

PAGES, DESIGN AND PAYMENTS

To set up the rest of your store, we need to create the pages you need, change the design of the site to suit you and add in how you will accept payments.

Creating Pages

We have a product or two in the store, we have our domain name and we have our email addresses. Now we want to make the store look like a proper store so we'll add some pages.

In your Shopify admin area click the "General" tab and go to the bottom of the page – a password is there, copy it and go back to your store webpage (the one with your domain name). Input that password.

Your store will look as it will to any visitor to it so look around, get the feel for it, click on stuff and make sure it all works. Once you have done that, you will have a better understanding of why you are going to be making the following changes.

We'll start with your front page; click on the prompt and you will go to your admin panel to the Pages section. Click on a page name and make some changes.

Input text as you would with any typing program. Give the customer a little information about you in your About Us page and also write what text is going to show up on the front page. Here, you can add other pages like a Contact Us page too.

Above the text window is a button for adding images; first, put your cursor in the position in the text you want the first image to appear and then click this button. Find your image (you should already have some saved on your computer for this). When you see the image in the window, click it and then click the box for "Size to Insert," choose the image size you want and then click the image icon again.

You will see that your image is in the text area, but none of the text wraps around it. If you want your image to show in between two paragraphs of text then you can leave this as it is but if you want the image within the text, we need to change it so click the image again and then click the Image icon.

Input a description for your image and then click the option to "Wrap Text Around Image." Add a little bit of spacing around your image – this will show as the white space between the text and the image.

Click on the button to "Edit Image," and you will see the text wrapped around your image with a nice white space separating it.

Go to the bottom of the area for text entry on the page and you will see some more fields to fill in – these are to do with the search engines, which will list websites that relate to the text content searched for by search engine users. Provide a description and a title – this is what is going to be seen in the search results when people look for you so make sure it is specific to the products or service you offer. You can leave the URL as is or provide a new one that uses good keywords. Lastly, click on "Save" and then on "Your Website>View" so you can see how your page looks.

Have a play around with the features on here and try adding other pages to the site. Once you are happy with what you have and are comfortable with creating pages, we'll move on to site design.

Changing Site Design

Your Shopify store is starting to take real shape now, but it still looks a bit, well plain and boring. Shopify provides you with the tools to create a stunning looking website with little effort and much of that is in the form of themes.

Go to your Shopify admin area and click on the "Themes" menu. Then click "Visit the Themes Store." On the left side of the store, choose "Free" and then choose any of the images to see information about a specific theme.

When you choose your theme, try to look beyond what you see in the product description; try to imagine your own store with the theme. Click the "View Demo" button to see the theme in action.

If you like it, you can see what it looks like on your own Shopify site. Close down the demo so you go back to the theme

44

store. Click "Get Theme" and then click on "Publish As My Shop Theme."

Next, click on "Go To My Theme Manager" and you can edit certain parts of the theme, like the colors and you can also images if the theme includes a header image or an image slider. Click "Customize Theme" and you will be directed to the Theme settings. As you make changes, click "Preview" to see them – this way you can decide as you go if your changes work or not.

You can add a logo and an icon if you have them on your computer. You can change colors, fonts and so on and you will find that every change is self-explanatory. You can change it back very easily if you find it doesn't work or you can even just go ahead and get a different theme.

When you are finished, click on "Save Changes." Don't be afraid to experiment and try several free themes. This will give you an idea of what works and what doesn't for your specific shop. If you feel like splashing out, you can also choose a paid theme. These can be filtered by industry and feature so you can find what you want quite easily. Do take care over choosing your theme though; it has to work and it has to do exactly what you want it to do. The alternative is hiring a web designer to create a custom website and that is not cheap.

Taking Payments

So, you have a fantastic store, filled to bursting with fantastic products and a stream of traffic just waiting to visit. All a waste of time unless you have a way to take their money and this is where we use Payment Providers. When the Internet first took off, the banks were too slow to come forward and offer good methods for online payments to businesses so, naturally, a number of other companies stepped up to the plate and filled the gap. These payment providers are what link the shopping cart to your bank. Check the Shopify website for more details about payment providers that work together with Shopify.

PayPal

PayPal is, without a doubt, one of the most tried and tested methods for taking payments, not to mention one of the securest and easiest. To use PayPal with your Shopify account you need to set up a PayPal Merchant Account. Shopify automates this so it isn't even necessary for you to have a PayPal account already set up. Shopify will let you know by email when a product has been paid for and to prompt you into setting your account up. If you do have an existing PayPal account, just click on "Edit" and input your PayPal email address.

Credit Card Payments

Not everyone uses or wants to use PayPal, indeed some countries restrict usage or don't support it at all. However, there are other options and one of those is credit card payments – for some customers, this is much easier and it can be more cost effective for you as well. If you want to avoid a scenario where a customer abandons their cart before they pay for it, it is well worth considering using more respected providers, such as Nochex. If you are in the UK.

In terms of fees, here's how the Nochex and PayPal fees differ:

- **PayPal** – 3.4% plus £0.02 per transaction. On a £10 sale, you would pay £0.54 to PayPal, while £100 sales would cost you £3.60 in fees

- **Nochex** – 2.9% plus £0.20 per transaction. A £10 sale would cost £0.49 while a £100 sale would cost £3.10.

Small savings but, in the long run, it adds up to a whole lot of savings.

To set up credit card payments, from your admin control panel, click on "Accept Credit Cards" and click on "Select Credit Card Gateway." Register your chosen service and use the same email address that you registered the service within the box provided.

Click on "Activate" and the service will begin working in your store.

It makes sense to offer a range of payment options to cater to all customers. Not everyone will want to add a credit card and not everyone will want to use PayPal either. Explore the options open to you in Shopify and choose the options that work for you.

CHAPTER 10

BEFORE YOU GO LIVE

Before your store can go live, there are a few more things you need to do, especially if your store is selling physical and not digital goods. Shipping rates need to be set, including postage and packaging and you need to let Shopify know how tax needs to be dealt with. You will also need to give your customers a way of contacting you in the case of returns or problems.

Shipping Rates and Order Fulfillment

To set your shipping rates, from your control panel, click on "Shipping." Input whatever locations and rates that you want but the easiest is to have two – a home country rate and then a "Rest of the World" rate.

Further down the page, there are options for adding Drop Shipping or Order Fulfillment. These are not Shopify services and are run by third parties – some of them very recognizable names. This is a great way of selling products across the whole world without needing to send packages yourself. You send the drop shipping company a load of your products and they do everything for you – storage of stock, packaging and posting. And, because Shopify will integrate easily with these services, your sales can be handled by the other company without you getting involved in the order.

Tax Rates

If you earn over a certain threshold in most countries, there are tax or VAT systems in place. If tax has to be added to orders, click on "Tax" in the main admin panel and input the correct tax amount in the box for "Country Tax Rate." This will then appear on invoices and you will be able to see the tax you collected in your sales reports. If you don't have to collect any tax, this value can just be set as zero.

To see tax reports, click on "Reports" and then on "Tax Rate."

Contact Details

If you don't provide your customers with a way of contacting you, they are not likely to buy from you. So, in the main menu, tap on "Settings" and input your store details. All relevant email addresses must be included. Click on "Save" when you have finished.

Refund, TOS and Privacy Statements

In your main menu, click on "Settings" and then click on "Checkout" at the bottom of the page, you can set policy statements for refunds, privacy and terms of service. To do this, just click on the button for "Generate Sample" and then use the generated statements or change them to suit your requirements.

Important note – make sure you do this ONLY after contact details have been input to ensure that the correct details go into the statements.

Payment Plans

Earlier we looked at the payment plans, now you need to choose one. By now you have had time to look at Shopify and see how it works and whether it will suit your business. If it does, go ahead and choose the plan you want.

Your store is now ready to go live. Check it over one more time to make sure and then remove that password – your store is now out in the wild and open for business.

CHAPTER 11

DO'S AND DON'TS

When you first start to use Shopify, there are a few things that you should be aware of, things to do and things that you should NOT do:

- DO make sure that your audience is properly targeted. If you do this, it's a pretty safe bet that your efforts will be reaching potential visitors that may convert to sales.

- DON'T design your shop website to be difficult for people to navigate. Not all of your audience will be tech-savvy and you can bet that they don't want to jump through hoops to get what they want. Keep it simple, not highly technical.

- DO add new content on a regular basis. Not only do customers like to see new products, so do the search engines. When your customers see the same old products every time they visit, they are liable to start looking elsewhere for their goods.

- DO use backlinks on your website where you can. How? Find an expert or authority on your specific niche and approach them about writing a guest post for them. You can add a couple of links without it looking like blatant advertising.

- DO learn about SEO or search engine optimization. Getting this right makes you far more visible in a good way on the internet.

- DO use the right keywords. They must fit naturally with your products and they must be appealing, drawing in users and making the search engines your friend.

- DO make each page on your website appealing to users. Customers can lad on any one of your pages and they want to see something great.

- DO think about using internal links to go to the different pages you have but do NOT make all your pages look like each other. Even more important, the homepage must be completely different from all the other pages.

- DO make your homepage look eye-catching with images – perhaps of your product being used by people. Also, use colors and link to the other pages on your websites.

- If your store also has a blog DO keep things simple. Your theme will likely have its own blog format so stick to using that. Your customers want to see great content otherwise they won't come back.

- DO try to use long tail search terms. These are the terms that users are likely to input into a search engine. For example, instead of searching for "winter boots," a person is likely to be more specific, perhaps "knee-length winter boots" or "winter boots with fur trim." By being more specific, a user is more likely to find what they want.

- DO use your blog. If you start it, finish it. Visitors don't like blogs that only have new content added on rare occasions. They want to see regular, high quality, unique and relevant content. They want you to entice them to buy and your blog posts should always ask the customer to make a purchase. If you can't commit to updating this regularly then don't start it in the first place.

As a final check before you do go live, run through this list and make sure that you can tick every one of them off as complete:

1. Have you chosen the plan that suits you the best?

2. Have you chosen and purchased a punchy domain name?

3. Have you chosen the right theme for your store?

4. Have you uploaded enough products?

5. Have you added your social media accounts?

6. Have you picked out the Shopify apps that will benefit you the most?

7. Is your store set up so it can take payments from customers?

8. Have you got all the hardware you require?
9. Have you worked out a marketing plan centered on social media?

If you have done everything and you are happy with the way your store looks, you are ready to go live.

BONUS CHAPTER

SHOPIFY AND AMAZON

Have you considered the benefits of integrating your Shopify store with Amazon? Let's face it, you really can't go too far wrong by using the largest online marketplace in the world and taking your brand to the next level. Shopify stores are great for showing off your brand and for offering a high level of control over the experiences your customers have. But for the right kind of business, using Amazon as a marketplace too can boost your sales by opening your store to a whole new audience.

The Benefits

The benefits of integrating Shopify and Amazon are numerous:

- You can create your listings on Amazon in multiple categories directly from Shopify

- If your products are on Amazon, you can create offers in any category directly from Shopify

- Your product details can be synced, as can images and variants, to your Seller Central account on Amazon

- Shopify products can be linked to existing listings on Amazon

- You can set prices and reserve a specific amount of inventory just for Amazon

- Shopify reports can be used to reconcile your Amazon revenue

- Shopify syncs tracked inventory data with Amazon

- Amazon orders can be fulfilled from Shopify

Using Shopify To Sell on Amazon

Following these steps, you can easily use Shopify to sell your products on Amazon:

First, you need to make sure that your Shopify store meets all the requirements:

- You must have a Shopify account signed up to any of the plans and it must be active

- The products you sell must fit into a category that is supported

- You must be able to list process in either CAD or USD

- You must not be making use of Fulfillment by Amazon to ship your goods

You can add any listings you already have on Amazon to your Shopify account even if they do not fall into a supported category.

The next step, if you don't have one already, is to create a Professional Seller account with Amazon and you can do this by going to Seller Central. You must also ensure that, regardless of which Amazon store you use, you can also sell on Amazon.com

It is free to add the sales channel, but your Professional Seller account will cost you $39.99 per month, plus referral fees, which are based on the category your product falls into. To get set up with an account:

- Go to Amazon Services and click the button that says, "Start Selling."

- Complete the details required – name, password, email address

- When the account has been created there are five steps to finish the setup. You will need to have certain information available:

  o Name, address and telephone number of your business

  o Credit card details for the monthly fee

  o Bank account details for sales revenue

  o TIN no (Tax ID No – US only)

- Once your account has been created, you need to make sure your product categories need to be <u>approved by Amazon</u>. If they do, you need to apply for it.

- Next, your Shopify store can be given the Sales Channel:

  - In Shopify, go to "Sales Channels" and click the + button next to it

  - Go to the "Amazon by Shopify" option and click on "Learn More"

  - Click on "Add Channel" and then on "Connect to Amazon."

  - Follow the on-screen prompts to get your Shopify and Amazon accounts integrated; when finished you will automatically go back to Shopify

- Most of the categories will require a product identifier so that sellers can create new pages for their products and list them on Amazon. A UPC is the most common, but if you don't provide one, or an ISBN or EAN, you will see an error message. At this point you will need to add in the required details to go any further. If your products are being resold (i.e., through affiliate marketing) you might find they already have that identifier and you can use that. If you do need to purchase one, the official UPC supplier is GS1, but there are other resellers that may do them a little cheaper.

- If this is your first time selling anything on Amazon, and your products are in the supported categories, you can go ahead and do your Amazon listing from in Shopify:

  o Go to "Amazon" and click it to find the sales channel you installed

  o Click on "Create Listing"

  o Look in your Shopify catalog to find the product you want and click on "Select Product."

  o If your product is your own brand, complete the details required in the box

  o If you are reselling and this is not your brand, click on "Search" and see if that same product has already been listed. If you see one in the list that matches your product, click on "Select" and create your Offer.

  o Complete all the required detail for whichever option you choose and then click on "Publish."

- If you have products on Amazon already, regardless of category, you can claim them in your Shopify store. Also, if you want to add products in categories not supported by Shopify, you can add them to Amazon and then you can add them to your store.

  Any listing that has been associated with your Amazon Professional account can be seen in your Shopify store under Amazon listings.

- o Click "Link Products" and find the listing you want to be linked.

- o Click "Browse Products" and look for the specific product, making sure you add the variants to your listing too.

- Now we need the tracking policy for the inventory. Every Amazon listing in your Shopify store needs one and you can choose between the store settings or manual management. If you opt for manual inventory management, you can reserve a portion of your stock purely for Amazon customers and, obviously, as each purchase is made, the inventory will drop and you will need to manually add more to it. Choosing the Shopify store settings, each product has a choice of three scenarios:

  - o Shopify will track your inventory

  - o Shopify will not track your inventory

  - o Customers may purchase products when they are out of stock.

Let's look a bit deeper into these options and how they work with your Amazon listings:

Shopify Will Track Your Inventory

If you opt for this, Shopify updates Amazon listings automatically so the total product inventory stored in Shopify is matched.

Shopify Will Not Track Inventory

If the inventory policy for any product is set as Don't Track, Shopify ensures that the product is always available on Amazon. The Amazon Seller Central account will show inventory as 100 for the product, but this will not appear in Shopify.

Amazon provides no support for unlimited quantities of products so you need to use 100 as a placeholder. Although it will decrease as products sell, every 10 minutes it will be updated back to 100.

Customers May Purchase Products When They Are Out of Stock

If you opt to allow customers to purchase when something is out of stock, Shopify ensures that the same product is available on Amazon. Again, the inventory is set as 100 for Amazon but won't appear in Shopify.

Important Note - Success on Amazon relied largely on positive reviews from your customers so do not sell stock on Amazon that is not available- people are very quick to leave negative reviews!

- Your final step is to get selling. Any orders made on Amazon sync automatically with the orders page on your Shopify store. Any new Amazon orders will show in your Orders list and will be marked as being Amazon sales accordingly. All orders are synced by Shopify, including those for products that have only been listed on Amazon.

- Customers will get their order notifications only from Amazon while you get them from Shopify too. If the order is not fulfilled through Shopify, it won't be updated.

Integrating Amazon and Shopify is easier than it looks and you won't regret doing it. Sales should receive a significant boost as your audience and target market is considerably wider.

BONUS CHAPTER

SHOPIFY AND FACEBOOK

As well as Amazon, it can greatly benefit you to integrate your Shopify store with your Facebook account, and any other social media account you have, Not only does this vastly improve the quality of your store, it also makes it more convenient for users and potentially boosts sales.

Some parts of the integration will make it far easier for you to advertise your store quickly and with less energy expended! Two examples are Facebook shop extensions and dynamic ads, which we'll talk about later. Other parts of the integration help to boost engagement with your store, build up trust with your customers and boost your sales. These are all benefits that you really can't afford to ignore if you want true success with your Shopify store.

Let's get started.

The first step is to install the Tracing Pixel provided by Facebook in your Shopify store. This pixel has two advantages – it tracks the activity of your users which allows you to use Facebook ads to retarget users and it also lets you know whether your Facebook ads are proving to be effective by providing details on clicks that result in conversions.

You don't need to have any coding experience to install the pixel as Shopify pretty much does it all for you. Here's how:

1. In your Facebook account, go to All Tools > Measure and Report > Pixels

2. Copy your Pixel ID number (write it down or highlight and copy)

3. Now go to your Shopify store and click on "Online Store."

4. Click on "Preferences" and go to the tab for "Facebook Pixel

5. Type in or paste your Pixel ID number – that's all you need to do and your pixel will be running immediately.

Using this method of installation, the tracking pixel will track these conversions automatically, with no coding required:

- AddPaymentInfo
- AddToCart
- InitiateCheckout
- Purchase

- Search

- ViewContent

The next step is to create and/or sync a Facebook shop with your Shopify store. Every business has the capacity to create Facebook shops where products can be directly sold via Facebook. If you have a Shopify Store, you can easily create a shop on Facebook that will sync with your Shopify store. This gives you two platforms for selling your products on and any inventory in Shopify is automatically updated to your Facebook shop at the time it updates on Shopify. You could, as you can with Amazon, choose to sell certain products on Facebook only and not have them show up in your Shopify store.

The best way to create your shop is to use the Facebook app in the Shopify store. It is a free app, but you must be using a paid package, as an absolute minimum, the $9 per month Lite Plan. Install the app and then, to set the shop up, you need your Facebook page connected.

If you have goods online already, Facebook reviews the shop and this can take up to two days to complete. Once Facebook has passed the review, your Shop can be enabled so goods can be published on Facebook.

You can also allow your customers the choice of checking out their cart on Shopify or, if their payment is in USD, to checkout using Facebook.

Next, dynamic ads can be set up. Don't avoid this step as you can use these ads to target customers who already looked at specific products on your site. Again, no coding is required because you can use an app to set the ads up and use the Pixel that you installed earlier:

- Go to the Shopify app store and get an app called Facebook Product Feed – the developer is Flexify. Once you install it, choose which products to include in the feed – to select a product it must be visible in your store.

- Next, click on "Native Shopify Pixel Setting" and choose "Format Feed."

- Copy the feed URL from the top of the page and go back to your Ads Manager on Facebook

- Click All Tools > Assets > Catalogs

- Creating a new catalog requires you to choose the product category so go ahead and do that and then choose which page your catalog will belong to and give the catalog a name

- Click on "Add Products"

- Choose how your data feed is going to be uploaded – click on "Set a Schedule" and input the feed URL you copied earlier. If you have a password protecting the feed, input the information

- Lastly, decide how to update the feed – hourly or weekly is best for dynamic ads

Your product feed is now ready and you can start running those dynamic ads.

Now, what we want to do next is choose to feature UGC in your Shopify store. UGC is User Generated Content and this goes a long way towards helping boost your sales. Much of this comes down to your visitors tending to trust people more than brands so, by adding a very prominent UGC that comes from your own social feeds, you can boost sales significantly.

There are a few Shopify as that can help you, including:

- Contentplum – 15-day free trial, $19.99 minimum per month

- Pixlee for Shopify- custom pricing

- Socialphotos – 30-day free trial, $10-$15 per month

Important Tip

By adding your social media accounts to your store, you are providing potential customers with a way of gaining access to your community online. This makes for a better relationship and lets visitors see information about your store before you go ahead and make a purchase.

There are a few apps that help you to add your social media icons to your storefront and these take visitors to each of your social accounts. One of the best free apps is called Social Media Tabs and, when installed in your store you can pick the icons you want on show, along with the icon color and their location in the store.

Don't ignore the power of Facebook and other social media accounts when it comes to boosting sales. Social media has the ability to reach much further and much wider than any other marketing strategy you might think of and they have been proven as effective and efficient ways to promote a business. Many of the top brands spend time and money on keeping their social media accounts up to date and to integrate with your Shopify account will maximize all the benefits you can gain.

CONCLUSION

Thanks for choosing this guide to read, I hope that it provided a helpful insight into how to set up and use Shopify to make money. You should now have a pretty good understanding of what Shopify is and what it can do for you.

It doesn't matter whether you are selling a few items to make money through a blog, are setting up a huge online store or even adding an online angle to your physical business, Shopify is the store to be in, offering plenty of tools and support to help you get your store up and running and be a success.

I hope that you are now ready to join the 'gold-rush' and choose Shopify as your way forward. It doesn't cost much to do and you can start small and see how things pan out before you make the leap and go big. If it doesn't work you haven't lost much so you really don't have anything to lose.

It will work though, provided you put the effort in and go for it.

Thank you for taking the time to read this guide and I wish you all the best in your Shopify venture.

www.ingramcontent.com/pod-product-compliance
Lightning Source LLC
Chambersburg PA
CBHW071441210326
41597CB00020B/3899